# 101 Salary Secrets

# 101 SALARY SECRETS
## *How to Negotiate*
## *Like a Pro*

Daniel Porot
and Frances Bolles Haynes

Ten Speed Press
Berkeley / Toronto

A Kirsty Melville Book

Ten Speed Press
P.O. Box 7123
Berkeley, California 94707
www.tenspeed.com

Distributed in Australia by Simon and Schuster Australia, in Canada by Ten Speed Press Canada, in New Zealand by Southern Publishers Group, in South Africa by Real Books, and in the United Kingdom by Airlift Book Company.

Cover and interior design by Larissa Pickens

Library of Congress Cataloging-in-Publication Data on file with the publisher.

ISBN 1-58008-230-0

First printing, 2000

Printed in Canada

3 4 5 6 7 8 9 10 — 08 07 06 05 04

**Authors' note: We have chosen to use masculine pronouns throughout this book. Using he/she, him/her and himself/herself would have made the text cumbersome and less readable. We have chosen to make the reading easier. Thank you for your understanding.**

# Contents

# Introduction

## NEGOTIATION: THE MOST MONEY YOU'LL EVER MAKE IN 3 MINUTES

In the advertising world, rates are often discussed in terms of cost per word. When training new employees to write copy, advertising professionals stress that each word is crucial, and therefore each word is valuable. The cost of an ad is divided by the number of words it contains. With this in mind, it is easy to see that the cost of one word in a four-color full-page ad is astronomical.

In salary negotiation just as with advertising copy, each second is crucial, and each can therefore be extremely valuable—if that second is spent negotiating effectively.

During a hiring interview, salary negotiation usually lasts less than three minutes, or 180 seconds. During this interview, you may negotiate the salary for a job in which you will spend years of your professional life. For this example, assume that you will spend five years in this job. If your annual salary is 100, the magnitude of your negotiation is 500 (100 x 5).

The cost of one second of negotiation is 500 divided by 180. (500/180 = 2.70 per second), as demonstrated in the table below.

| *For a job where you stay 5 years, with an annual salary of:* | *On a basis of 3 minutes, one second of negotiation is worth (5 x salary/180):* |
| --- | --- |
| $30,000. . . . . . . . . . . . | $833 |
| $50,000. . . . . . . . . . . . | $1,389 |
| $75,000. . . . . . . . . . . . | $2,083 |
| $100,000. . . . . . . . . . . | $2,778 |

Figure out the cost of one second of negotiation for the salary you want using the table below.

_____ x 5 = _____ / 180 = _____
*Write the annual salary you desire. Multiply by 5 (approximate number of years you will spend in the job). This will give you the anticipated salary for 5 years. Divide this figure by the 180 seconds that negotiation usually lasts. This is the cost of one second of negotiation.*

In the job-hunting process, and more precisely during the hiring interview, salary negotiation is brief and has significant consequences. It is vitally important to prepare well for it, avoid jumping into it too fast, and conduct it with a good knowledge of negotiation techniques.

*101 Salary Secrets: How to Negotiate Like a Pro* will arm you with the knowledge you need to enter into salary negotiation with confidence—and to come out a winner! Just like negotiation itself, this book is brief, designed to maximize each second you spend preparing to negotiate. The strategies and advice given here are simple, straightforward, and effective. They are presented as concisely as possible to give you the information you need efficiently, allowing you to prepare for an interview overnight, if necessary. To make the most of this book and to get the best possible preparation, we suggest that you read the book thoroughly one time. Stop and practice the sample dialogs in front of a mirror as you read. When you are finished, go back through the book and review the 101 most important points—our 101 Salary Secrets. They are highlighted throughout the book using this symbol:

To refresh your memory before the interview, flip through the book, reading only these 101 points and practicing the dialogs. We believe you'll find the system presented here to be the easiest, fastest way to prepare for a salary negotiation interview. Good luck, and happy negotiating!

*Chapter 1*

# The Right Attitude

# In This Chapter

Dispelling Myths

Are You Really Worth That?

Getting into a Positive Frame of Mind

You've no doubt heard the phrase "It's all in the attitude." Nowhere is this more true than in salary negotiation. Hiring managers can smell fear. If you display uncertainty, insecurity, or a lack of confidence, your leverage in negotiation is substantially weakened. To succeed, you must project a positive self-image, one that says boldly, "This is the salary I want, and I am worth every penny!"

For most job candidates, salary negotiation is a very uncomfortable subject. Both our educational process and natural shyness help account for this. Additionally, when you have been unemployed for a long time the idea of being back in a job can be so attractive you often are not willing to jeopardize your chances of getting hired because of a salary issue. You are ready to accept any salary just to get back into a job.

An interviewer knows this and may take advantage of it. Although some interviewers will use this leverage unscrupulously, others will simply employ good negotiation tactics to minimize costs—that is their job. Whatever the case, arming yourself with knowledge and dispelling myths surrounding salary negotiation can help you maintain the confidence and poise you must project to succeed.

*Myth: Everything the interviewer says
      is true.*

*Myth: Exceptions do not exist.*

# DISPELLING MYTHS

Strong myths exist about salary negotiation. They are being kept alive by both job candidates who are unsure of themselves and by unscrupulous interviewers who want to take advantage of candidates. Nothing we discuss in this book will help you if you believe any of the following myths. One of the best things you can do to arm yourself with the confidence necessary for effective negotiation is to be aware of the following myths and dispel them from your mind!

**Myth: Everything the interviewer says is true.** Like you, an interviewer bargains. He holds on to as much information as possible and releases the facts in a sequence that suits him. In the process, he will allow you to believe things that may be untrue—if you let him!

#1

**Myth: Exceptions do not exist.** In an extreme situation, an organization can always break the rules and make exceptions on salary amounts. If they really need you, they will find tangible means to convince you to join them.

#2

*Myth: Lowering your expectations increases your chances of getting the job.*

*Myth: The first figure is often a good one.*

*Myth: Salaries are never negotiable.*

**Myth: Lowering your expectations increases your chances.** Insecure behavior consists of undervaluing yourself—or worse—lowering your salary expectation without asking for something in return. Stick to your guns! It will earn you respect and may even increase your chances of being hired.

**Myth: The first figure is often a good one.** One of the most common errors made is to believe that you have to accept the first offer made to you during the negotiation . . . because you fear it will be the only offer. Actually, the first offer is a starting point, one of the two defining points that establish the range. Remember, if they want to hire you, they will negotiate.

**Myth: Salaries are never negotiable.** Salaries are most always negotiable. If an organization needs and wants you, they will negotiate. Some interviewers may try to avoid discussing salary. If there is no discussion, there is no negotiation. Be prepared to insist on negotiating!

*A good negotiation has two winners: the employer must be convinced he has made a good decision, and you must be equally satisfied.*

*To maintain the proper confident attitude, be prepared to generate a win-win situation by justifying yourself economically.*

## ARE YOU REALLY WORTH THAT?

In a successful negotiation, not only must you be satisfied with your salary, but you must also convince the interviewer that he is paying a fair price and that you are getting the right salary.

A good negotiation is when there are two winners. In the case of a hiring negotiation, both employer and employee need to have the feeling that they have made a good deal.

#6

- The employer has to be convinced that he has made a good decision. For him, the amount that he will pay as salary has to appear like a sound and profitable investment.

- The employee (you) has to be equally satisfied. The amount which will be paid to you has to appear as a fair and honest compensation for the work you will do.

To ensure this balance, and to conduct the negotiation with the proper confident attitude, you must be prepared to justify yourself economically.

#7

*Understand at the outset, the interviewer sees you as "a guaranteed cost" and "an uncertain contribution."*

Remember, initially the employer sees you as *a guaranteed cost,* but only as *an uncertain contribution:*

- You are "a guaranteed cost," since he will have to set aside and pay you a salary and other expenses at the end of each month;

- And you are an "an uncertain contribution," since he cannot be certain ahead of time that the work you perform will generate enough positive results to justify your expense to the organization.

To make an argument for the salary you believe fair, it is extremely helpful if you can quantify your contribution in some way. You must show, for instance, that your contribution can:

1. Increase profits by:

   - developing sales;

   - discovering new customers;

   - opening new channels of distribution.

2. Decrease costs by:

   - reorganizing systems to decrease processing time;

*Be prepared to quantify your contribution by demonstrating that you can help increase profits, decrease costs, and avoid errors. List three to five ways your skills can make positive, concrete contributions in these areas.*

- training personnel in efficiency;

- developing systems to avoid duplication.

3. Avoiding errors by:

- writing water-tight contracts;

- selecting better equipment;

- preventing accidents.

Spend some time thinking about the ways your skills can make positive, concrete contributions to your employer's organization. Make a list with three columns at the top, one for each of the three categories listed above. Try to come up with at least three to five specific ways that you will contribute to the organization in your prospective position. The more concrete ideas you have of how you will contribute to the company, the more justified you will feel in asking for the salary you deserve. In addition, you will have specifics to offer during the negotiation process as you help the interviewer to feel more confident that your "uncertain contribution" will be positive. In other words, you will be able to demonstrate that you are "a resource person" and not "a job beggar"—an image that is essential not only for

*Remember that you have their interest.*

your own self-confidence, but also for the employer's peace of mind. The more you succeed in convincing them of this, the more you are perceived as an answer to their problems. You will become unique and memorable compared to other applicants. The criteria the interviewer will use to judge you will not be age, sex, or degree, but your aptitude to solve their problems. Finally, the more effective you are in projecting this image, the more likely you will be able to frame the salary negotiation as a win-win scenario.

## GETTING INTO A POSITIVE FRAME OF MIND

As you prepare for an interview, the following points can help you feel more at ease.

**Remember that you have their interest.** You clearly have the capacity to carry out the work needed to do the job, otherwise you would not have been invited to come for an interview.

#10

*Remember that you have been chosen.*

*Convince yourself that you will succeed.*

*Be determined.*

*Gather information.*

*Listen and make them talk.*

**Remember that you have been chosen.** You have been chosen among other candidates. This is a very positive sign and should bolster your self-confidence.

**Convince yourself you will succeed.** The decision of an interviewer is based 95 percent on your personality, enthusiasm, and skills. These factors will help you negotiate your salary.

**Be determined.** By being determined and firm you will increase your own value. You can increase your chances of getting hired—and of getting the salary you want—by demonstrating that you know what you want.

**Gather information.** You project the image of a professional when you have a good knowledge of the world of work and salaries. The information in Chapter 3 is a great place to start!

**Listen and make them talk.** Your negotiation capacity depends upon your listening capacity. A basic rule of listening is to let the other person explain his

#11

#12

#13

#14

#15

*Explain things even if they seem obvious.*

*Repeat your presentation.*

*Take your time.*

point of view thoroughly and only then for you to enter the conversation. As long as you have not gathered all the information needed, do not take sides, judge, or give your final point of view. Also, learn to be comfortable with silence. Interviewers will often employ silence as a way of getting you to talk. If you need more information, ask for it, and wait in silence until they have thoroughly explained what you need to know.

**Explain things even if they seem obvious.** What is obvious to you is not always obvious to your interviewer. Take the time and care to explain your position using simple logic and convincing facts and figures.

#16

**Repeat your presentation.** Use repetition as a negotiation tool. When you reinforce a point, do it in a different way each time and provide the interviewer with quantified proof of your achievements.

#17

**Take your time.** Postpone the time when you might need to compromise. When a proposal suits you, take twice as much time as needed to accept it.

#18

*Prepare yourself thoroughly.*

**Prepare yourself thoroughly.** Preparing yourself for negotiation does not consist of learning "canned" or rote answers. To prepare yourself, pay attention to the three following points:

- Have a very clear-cut idea of the statements that you wish to use to convince them of your value.

- Plan beforehand the sequence in which you will use these statements.

- Learn how to present them in the best possible way. Chapters 4 and 5 will offer specific principles and strategies for negotiation, including sample dialogs illustrating how to use them.

Remember, there is almost always something that can be negotiated in your favor. If you are one of the lucky ones, however, you may get exactly what you want and will not have the need to negotiate anything. If you feel the salary you will get is fair and the benefits are just what you wanted, you can smile all the way home from your interview. Keep in mind that you do not have to negotiate just for the sake of negotiating. What counts is that you are satisfied with what you get!

*Chapter 2*

# Timing Is Everything: The Interview Curve

# In This Chapter

The Interview Curve

The Seven Stages of an Interview

Buy Signals: 40 Positive Signs

You have picked a daisy to play the famous game, "He loves me, he loves me not…." When an interviewer "loves you not," the appropriate time to negotiate a salary has not arrived. It is only when "he loves you" that you must jump into the negotiation process. Don't miss the right time! "He loves me" and "he loves me not" are very close to each other, and it is easy to take a wrong step at the wrong time.

*Get a good sense of when to negotiate
by knowing the stages of an interview.*

# THE INTERVIEW CURVE

Paul Hellman, author of *Ready, Aim, You're Hired!* (American Management Association, 1986), offers a wonderful visual illustration of the stages of a job interview that indicates the best time to begin salary negotiation. He uses a curve plotted along two axes. The vertical axis shows the most favorable conditions for negotiating salary. The higher up the axis you are, the better the conditions for negotiation. The horizontal axis serves as the "time line."

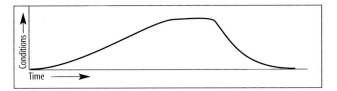

The curve is divided into three sections: ascension, plateau, and descent. These represent the trajectory of stages during a typical hiring interview.

**A. The Ascension section** corresponds to the period of the interview when you are demonstrating that you are the right person for the job. It corresponds

*The best time to negotiate is when you are on the "plateau" of the interview curve—not before and not after.*

to stages 1 through 4 of the "Seven Stages of an Interview" outlined on the following pages.

This phase may sometimes be short and could take place during the first interview. When this is the case, it usually lasts from ten to thirty minutes. In other instances this phase is much longer and can be spread over several interviews.

**B. The Plateau section** is usually very short and indicates the best time for salary negotiation. It corresponds to stages 5 and 6 of the "Seven Stages of an Interview" outlined on the following pages.

**C. The Descent section** is very steep and illustrates your slide into failure. It will take you down a road you don't wish to travel. There is almost nothing you can do to stop the descent once you have left the plateau section and missed your chance to negotiate. The descent section corresponds to stage 7 of the "Seven Stages of an Interview."

The art of negotiation consists in approaching salary negotiation only when you are on the plateau—not before, and not after.

#21

*To progress through Stage 1, focus on characteristics and achievements that set you apart from other candidates.*

# THE SEVEN STAGES
# OF AN INTERVIEW

To seize your opportunity to negotiate at the right time, be aware of the seven stages of an interview. These stages can be found in just one interview, or they can be spread over several interviews. Your success will depend on how well you have prepared for the interview, your polish and professionalism, and the quality of your answers to the interviewer's questions. For advice on interviewing, see our previous book, *The 101 Toughest Interview Questions . . . and Answers that Win the Job!*

For our purposes here, we will assume the interview is going very well, and you are moving smoothly through the stages on your way to negotiating the salary for your new job.

**Stage 1: "Who are you?"** At the beginning of the interview, the first question the interviewer asks you (directly or indirectly) is "Who are you?" This stage can be very short (about ten minutes) or very long (two to four hours).

#22

*Prove "you are not so bad" by giving brief answers that highlight relevant achievements that match the interviewer's needs.*

Do not answer this question by providing personal characteristics, such as age, marital status, or degrees. Focusing on personal characteristics is a bad strategy because it pushes the interviewer to compare you to other candidates and prevents you from being seen as a unique person. Select from among your past achievements and experiences the things of interest to your interviewer that make you different from others, and therefore unique. Focus on skills and achievements with direct relevance to the position for which you are interviewing. This will ensure you move to the next stage.

**Stage 2: "You are not so bad."** Focusing on relevant achievements from your past that truly match the interviewer's needs will draw your interviewer to the conclusion that "you are not so bad." Your interviewer, usually very careful and cautious at the beginning of the interview, will become more positive if your answers directly correlate to his needs. By being selective with your answers and being brief (from twenty seconds to two minutes per statement) you will impress the interviewer and move to the next stage.

#23

The interviewer's attitude toward you will become more and more positive as you demonstrate that you have the skills for the job and a good track record implementing those skills.

As the interviewer's attitude shifts, he will stop trying to weed you out and begin encouraging you to paint a flattering picture of yourself. Oblige him! But it's not yet time to start negotiating...

**#24**

**Stage 3: "You look good."** If you are able to present enough personal achievements to demonstrate that you can perform the job and that you also have a personal history of performing similar responsibilities exceptionally well, the interviewer will move toward thinking that "you look good." From one candidate among many, you will become more and more "unique" and will proceed to the next stage. Although there is no clear-cut way to know exactly what stage you are in at any given moment, you should pay close attention to the interviewer's attitude and body language. As his reactions to your statements begin to seem more and more positive, you can feel confident that you are making progress through the stages.

**#25**

**Stage 4: "We must hire you."** As the positive momentum of the interview builds, every additional achievement or characteristic you discuss about yourself will be seen in a more and more positive light. The interviewer may even begin asking "easier" questions designed not to "weed you out," but to allow you to paint the most flattering picture of yourself possible. The winds are begin-

*Pay careful attention to your interviewer's words, attitude, and body language. At this stage, he will begin to broadcast "buy signals." Watch for these signals: they reveal that the interviewer is ready to make an offer—and is afraid he might lose you to the competition!*

ning to shift, and the interviewer is becoming convinced that "we must hire you."

At this stage of the interview, the feelings of your interviewer are moving beyond simple interest in you as a job candidate and becoming tinged with the anxiety that accompanies the next stage—the anxiety of losing you to the competition!

**Stage 5: "I can't let the competition get him."** When you come to this stage, you will no longer be a "stranger" to your interviewer but someone who he is actively trying to welcome "into the fold." He may even begin treating you as if you are already a member of his corporate family. From here on, you belong to his universe.

As a stronger anxiety grows in the interviewer that he might "lose you to the competition," you will leave the rational world to step into an irrational one—the one in which your negotiation tactics are most likely to succeed. You are nearing the plateau!

Feeling scared, he will likely begin to "tip his hand" and show his real feelings about you. His behavior will become less and less formal and he will broadcast "buy signals." It is now up to you to notice them.

#26

When you have observed at least three "buy signals," you are on the plateau. The timing is right for salary negotiation.

Don't postpone the negotiation too long. If the interviewer can't solve his problem by hiring you immediately, he will begin to look for other ways to solve it!

**#27**

**Stage 6: "The Plateau."** It is only when you are on the plateau that you can start negotiating your salary without taking risks. If you try to negotiate salary during the ascension phase, your interviewer has not made the decision to hire you yet and your negotiation power is weak. The trick is not to discuss salary until you are certain the interviewer has made the decision to hire you. Otherwise, your salary demands themselves may factor into his hiring decision. "Oh, he's asking too much, so I won't pursue him any further," he may think. If you are on the plateau, however, he has already decided he wants you. He is much more likely at this stage to be flexible with salary offers: he'll want to do anything he can to get you on board!

To determine if you have reached the plateau you must identify at least three signs which show that your interviewer is ready to hire you. You can then begin to negotiate salary with confidence. Examples of these signs, or "buy signals," are listed later in this chapter.

**#28**

**Stage 7: "Too late."** If you don't start salary negotiation when you are on the plateau, or if you wait too long, your interviewer may think you are not interested in the

*Be sure to evaluate buy signals in context—that is, pay attention to how the interview "feels." If the buy signals match this positive feeling, they are probably genuine.*

job. He also may find a number of alternative candidates in the meantime who he'll "settle for" if your negotiation doesn't go well, giving him a kind of safety net.

One of the key criteria for a job candidate for most interviewers is enthusiasm. By postponing salary negotiation too long, he may think that you are not interested, or that you are "holding out" for other job offers. Either way, you will have missed your best window of opportunity for negotiating.

## BUY SIGNALS: 40 POSITIVE SIGNS

You will identify the most appropriate time to negotiate salary by recognizing positive signs or "buy signals" from the interviewer. Examples of these are clustered here in four categories. It is possible, of course, for some of these signs to arise in an interview and not constitute buy signals. Each must be evaluated in context. If you feel confident that you are at or approaching stage 6 of your interview—that is, if you feel you have made a good impression, that you've "clicked" with the interviewer, and that his attitude has become increasingly more positive—then you are probably quite right to interpret the following as buy signals.

#29

*Know how to recognize buy signals expressed as questions.*

*Know how to recognize buy signals expressed as behaviors.*

**Signs Expressed as Questions**

The interviewer:

- tries to obtain details about your non-competitive clause and how much notice you must give to leave your present job;

- tries to find out if you have other job offers;

- asks, "When can you start?";

- asks about your preferences for a company car;

- asks very specific questions about your job references;

- questions you to see if you really like or want the job;

- asks whether you would move or be willing to commute every day.

**Signs Expressed as Behaviors**

The interviewer:

- has "a partner in crime" look;

- behaves more warmly and appears more relaxed;

*Know how to recognize buy signals
expressed as a "sales pitch."*

- gets closer physically to you, reduces the distance and space between the two of you;

- sits on the same side of the desk/table as you;

- starts talking faster and more excitedly;

- leaves the room for a few minutes;

- does not question your past further;

- shares confidential files with you.

### Signs Expressed as a Sales Pitch

The interviewer:

- describes the fringe benefits of his company;

- tells you he has discussed your application with a key person in the organization;

- discusses ways you can convince the final decision maker to hire you;

- shares company gossip with you;

- increases the number of compliments he gives you;

- makes a salary offer that "you cannot turn down";

**#32**

*Know how to recognize buy signals
expressed in other ways.*

- mentions that you are one of only two candidates still under consideration;
- describes additional means/perks he will "throw into the pot";
- asks you to accept the limitations of the job (a small office, a shared computer);
- is much more willing to answer your questions;
- suggests that you start working with him immediately;
- discusses the advantages of the area (schools, shops, recreation facilities).

**Other Signs**

The interviewer:

- says, "You will see" (implying you will be coming on board);
- starts using his calculator;
- uses the word "when" instead of "if";
- uses the word "we" instead of "you";

#33

- gets the Human Resource Manager;
- invites you to visit the company headquarters or plant facility;
- takes you to your future office;
- invites you for lunch/dinner;
- offers you something to drink;
- introduces you to key people in the organization;
- has you meet "Mr. X" (stating he is the one to make the final decision);
- introduces you to your future subordinates.


- Finally, the interviewer's secretary/assistant becomes friendlier.

_Chapter 3_

# The Nuts and Bolts
# of Salaries

# In This Chapter

All jobs comprise different elements that make them attractive or unattractive to a particular individual. It is important to determine if the elements in a given job will fit your needs. If you do not have a good "mix," it is unlikely that you will take the job or stay in the job long if you do accept it. So, before discussing salary in an interview, you need to discuss and understand four other elements first.

*The four elements of the "job mix" are important because they will affect your job satisfaction and your salary expectations.*

*Find out the scope of your responsibilities in your new job.*

*You must know what factors will affect future advancement potential.*

# THE JOB MIX

The four "job mix" elements are important not only because they will affect your overall job satisfaction, but also because they will directly affect your salary expectations (and therefore your salary negotiations). Before discussing salary, then, you must establish:

**#34**

**1. The scope of your responsibilities.** What will your exact responsibilities be in terms of people and equipment under your supervision, budget concerns, etc.? Obviously, the greater your responsibility, the higher your salary expectations will be.

**#35**

**2. Your chances to be promoted.** What are your chances to advance? Will your next promotion be lateral or vertical? Are promotions more often made from within the company or from without? How quickly might you expect to move up? Occasionally it may be worth accepting a lower salary if you can reasonably expect to be promoted with a pay increase in a relatively short time. If the promotional structure is more rigid, however, or if advancement opportunities are fewer, your starting salary will be all the more important.

**#36**

*Training opportunities in your new job may give it added value for you.*

*Know the structure of the company hierarchy before accepting a position or a salary.*

**3. The training opportunities.** What type of training will the company offer you? Will this training relate only to your future job with the company, or will it contribute to your overall personal or professional development? The opportunity to receive training and acquire new skills can be an intangible benefit to any job—adding to its overall personal value for you.

**4. The company hierarchy.** To whom will you report? Who will be your boss? Who will evaluate your efforts and successes? Are you comfortable with this structure? The number of people above and below you can also help give you an idea of the promotional opportunities and the scope of your responsibilities relative to the company as a whole.

#37

#38

*Salary is just one component of your com-
pensation package. Your salary may be
based on a fixed amount, a variable
amount, or both.*

# THE COMPENSATION PACKAGE

Just as it is important to know the "job mix" before discussing salary with an interviewer, you must also have a good understanding of the nature and structure of salaries themselves. A salary is just one part of your overall "compensation package." Just as the four elements of the "job mix" can increase or decrease the "value" of the job as a whole, there are components of compensation packages other than salary that can make a job offer more or less attractive.

Any compensation package includes both a salary and benefits. The salary can be broken down into:

**#39**

- Only a fixed amount;

- Only a variable amount (commission and bonuses directly proportional to the efficiency of the individual and/or his department);

- A fixed amount and a variable amount.

*Distinctions can be made between net, gross, or total salary. Be sure you know which is being discussed during a negotiation!*

Benefits can be broken down into:

> • Financial (profit sharing, expense accounts, etc.);
>
> • Tangible (car, apartment, etc.);
>
> • Intangible (leave of absence, vacation time, training events, insurance packages, etc.).

A more comprehensive list of benefits is given later in this chapter.

## NET, GROSS, AND TOTAL

In addition to the three types of salaries discussed above, there are three ways of talking about salaries: net, gross, and total. In any negotiation it is important to know how these distinctions affect both you and your employer—and it's quite important to know exactly which one is being discussed during negotiation!

**The Net Salary**. This is your "take-home pay," the amount you get at the end of each period after your employer has deducted any charges you must pay. For example, if your gross salary is 100, your net salary may

*Even though benefits may not increase your actual salary, from your employer's perspective, they contribute substantially to your overall cost to the company— perhaps thousands of dollars a month!*

be only 80 after social security payments, insurance premiums, etc. You may also have to distinguish between net salary before taxes and net salary after taxes. In the latter case, your employer withholds the taxes to pay the tax authorities.

**The Gross Salary.** To figure your gross salary, combine your net salary (the amount you receive at the end of each pay period) and any charges you are compelled to pay (social security, insurance, etc.).

**The Total Salary.** This is the total amount that you cost your employer. In other words, it is your gross salary plus any other charges that your employer is compelled to pay for you.

For example, if your gross salary is 100, your total salary may be as high as 120 to 140. This extra amount reflects the charges that are paid by your employer directly to official bodies (social security, retirement, insurance, etc.) on your behalf.

#41

*Before negotiating, find out whether or not your company uses salary curves, indexes, or points.*

# HOW SALARIES ARE BUILT

Some companies or public organizations have a compensation system which is based on salary curves, an index system, or points. A main goal of a salary curve is to establish consistency between all the employees in an organization. This consistency limits injustice, and eliminates potential sources of conflict.

Another way to compute salaries is to base them on points. In a given organization a certain number of tasks is defined for each job. Those tasks are coded and each task is allocated a certain number of points. By adding up all the points allocated to each task of a job, you get a total number called an "index": the higher the index, the higher the salary.

# GET THE BEST OF
# THOSE SALARY CURVES

Often the very fact that a company has a salary curve or an index system limits the ability of the interviewer (and you) to negotiate salary. Negotiation is possible, however, by using one of the following strategies.

*To beat a salary curve, try to negotiate additional responsibilities that will increase your position on the curve.*

*Try to change curves altogether by having your employer enrich the content of your job.*

*To get around salary curves, try to negotiate other sources of income, such as bonuses and overtime pay.*

**Strategy 1: Gain a few additional points**. Try to modify the position of your job on the curve by mentioning anything that can add value to your application, such as: education, experience of XX years, or a very specific skill or knowledge that will allow you to take on additional tasks in your position.

**Strategy 2: Change Curves.** Have your employer redefine and enrich the content of your job so that it will be positioned on a higher curve.

For example, if your job is to be positioned on Curve 6, make a list of every task you must do. Eliminate some of the tasks and add new tasks which enrich your job and give you more responsibilities. Hence, instead of being positioned on Curve 6, your job is now positioned on Curve 8!

**Strategy 3: Look for Bonuses.** Try to have additional responsibilities included in your job description, or to negotiate a schedule for bonuses based on hours logged or work produced. This may generate additional sources of income such as overtime, or special bonuses, which will generate a bigger paycheck.

*Negotiating benefits is an often overlooked way to increase your overall compensation package. It is also a useful way to get around the obstacle of a salary curve.*

**Strategy 4: Negotiate Benefits.** If any of the three strategies mentioned above does not apply, you can undertake "Plan B" and accept a lower salary than the one you originally anticipated. However, fill in this gap with some sort of advantage that:

- does not cost (or has a small cost) to your employer but means a lot to you;

- cannot become the general rule for other employees. When a company wants to hire you, they are often willing to give you anything you ask for, provided it does not set a precedent that others will try to use.

- is not perceived as "one-upmanship" by your future colleagues.

Benefits can be an excellent negotiation strategy for several reasons:

- they are an excellent way to keep a situation from getting stuck;

*Benefits can mean much more than health insurance. Familiarize yourself with the list of benefits provided to get creative ideas for other ways to improve your compensation package.*

• they allow you to fill in the gap between what the company is able to offer and what you want to get;

• they are often tax free.

Here is a comprehensive list of benefits that may be used in negotiation. Some are very common; some others are very unusual:

## 47

- Admissions to associations, clubs, shows;

- Possibility to barter;

- Special insurance;

- Free use of company assets (boat, plane, chalet, etc.);

- Yearly medical check-up;

- Special financial commission on deals for which you are responsible;

- Paid (or unpaid) leave of absence;

- Training courses;

- Special loans with little or no interest;

- Job for a relative;

- Education assistance for children;
- Special work schedule (time);
- Board of Directors compensation;
- Paid day off (long weekend) against overtime;
- Time off to do community service work;
- Housing (total or partial assistance);
- Vacation house;
- Special equipment at your disposal (computers, telephone, cellular phone, etc.);
- Special assignments in other branches/subsidiaries for extra compensation;
- Overtime paid;
- Golden parachute (bonus for leaving before actual retirement date);
- Bodyguard or security systems;
- Parking;
- Equity/stock;
- Profit sharing;
- Additional points to add value to the salary curve;

- Possibility to buy company products at cost (or get them free);

- Possibility to work for the organization as a consultant after retirement;

- Bonus for joining;

- Reimbursement of specific expenses (entertainment, books, etc.);

- Transfer of retirement benefits to new position;

- Company cafeteria at cost (or free);

- Salary revision every six months;

- Additional secretarial/administrative support;

- Waiver of trial period;

- Additional retirement benefits (matching contributions to retirement funds);

- Pay for home telephone (partial or total);

- Car;

- Free travel for spouse on business trips.

*Offering to become a consultant is another way to get outside restrictive salary curves and to receive the compensation you want.*

If you have to move for a new job, listed here are some benefits that you can negotiate.

- Financing the costs of the move;
- Hotel costs for house hunting time;
- Pay prepayment mortgage penalty;
- Pay commission of real estate agent;
- Pay difference between previous rent/mortgage and new rent/mortgage;
- Buy your old house;
- Pay to remodel your new house.

In the time of so many business start-ups, you might also consider negotiating for a percentage of ownership in a company, or a share of the equity, in lieu of a high salary. This is a very specific and risky kind of negotiation and should probably involve advice from a lawyer.

**Strategy 5: Become a Consultant.** If the company does not have the capability to offer you the kind of salary you are looking for without jeopardizing its internal climate, offer to become a consultant. In this case there will be no salary paid, only fees. When you act as a consultant, you can negotiate fees two to three times higher than a salary.

#48

*Consult published salary surveys to get an idea of what salary range is realistic for you.*

In this way, the internal climate of the organization is not at risk. No one can realistically claim that salaries are unfair.

## SCOUT IT OUT BEFORE YOU GO: SALARY SURVEYS

**#49**

In addition to knowing how salaries are structured in terms of salary curves, compensation packages, and benefits, it is useful before negotiating to have a general idea of what other people in similar jobs are being paid in your industry.

Many data collecting organizations (professional associations in a particular field, alumni associations, unions, lobbying groups, etc.) and even popular magazines and business newspapers often undertake salary surveys to determine the level of salaries in a specific job. For example, the medical industry may undertake a survey to determine the national pay scale range for first-year residents. By contacting the American Medical Association, either in person or via the Internet, a job hunter can get a copy of their salary survey.

*Mentioning salary surveys can be helpful to both you and the employer. Use them to create win-win outcomes.*

Job hunters today are fortunate to have a tool like the Internet to help them gather information before attending an interview. The Internet allows you to find all kinds of information in a fraction of the time it used to take to locate such facts and figures. While it may still be useful to contact companies and other organizations directly to get specific kinds of information, the Internet provides a fast, easy way to obtain basic information or at least suggestions of other groups to contact. Thanks to the Internet, in less than ten or twenty minutes, you can attend an interview having done your homework first. And doing this homework will allow you to have an advantage when it comes to salary negotiation.

Salary surveys are interesting to study from the standpoint of both the employer and the employee.

**For you, consulting a salary survey can:**

- Help avoid surprises;
- Give you a benchmark to begin salary negotiation;
- Inform you about the limitations of any field (the top and the bottom of the range);
- Increase your self-confidence;

**#50**

- Prevent you from mentioning your (too low) former salary;
- Help you understand how a company evaluates a job in a specific field;
- Give you an indication of a company or a field's health and philosophy;
- Tell you if a company is generous or greedy.

**For an employer, consulting a salary survey can:**

- Let him know if his personnel are correctly paid;
- Help him to budget;
- Give him an indication of his position in the market;
- Help him establish a salary index;
- Help him to assess the value of new positions being created;
- Limit the number of claims and complaints;
- Allow him to attract good candidates by knowing what to offer.

*Use other resources, such as the Internet, to refine the information you get from published surveys.*

## 51

# REFINE AND EXPAND THE SURVEY

In addition to published salary surveys, listed here are ways of obtaining supplemental salary information to help you narrow down the salary range that will apply to you in your specific area and field. Using these additional resources is important because they can help you determine whether the information you find in salary surveys accurately applies to the particular position you are seeking.

- Study employment ads that specify salary;

- Approach unions, professional associations, alumni associations, etc.;

- Use resource centers (career centers) at universities or colleges;

- Consult state and federal placement offices;

- Ask headhunters and temporary agencies;

- Question friends and relatives.

*You can also perform your own informal salary survey while conducting informational interviews.*

# CONDUCT YOUR OWN SALARY SURVEY

## 52

Most people in today's job market are familiar with the concept of informational interviews. This concept was first discussed in Richard N. Bolles's book, *What Color Is Your Parachute?* and further outlined in Daniel Porot's book, *The PIE Method.* Basically, this method of preparing for a job interview and subsequent salary negotiation suggests that you conduct interviews "for information only" with people in your field of interest. You might approach an individual for a fifteen to twenty minute interview to gather information about the specific job: how to get into the job, its pluses, minuses, tasks, skills needed, etc. You may also ask the kind of salary range for the job, but at no time during this informational interview do you ask for or accept a job. This is a preparatory stage only; you should use it only to gather information to determine whether a particular job/field/industry (and its salary) suits you.

After finding out the basic facts about a job, you might ask the person: "If I were to be in the type of job you have, could you please give me a very broad idea— say within 30 percent—of the sort of salaries people are paid in your field?" Another way of saying it could be: "During my preceding informational interviews, the most common salary figures for this type of job ran between _____ and _____ (provide a very wide range). Do you think that this range is representative in your field?"

When you ask for this kind of information, it is helpful to tell those you ask that you are conducting an informal salary survey and that you will share the results with them when you have concluded it. Most people will be interested to know what others in their field are making.

After a few interviews, you will get relatively specific information. However, because your sample is narrow, it is only indicative of the *range* of salaries and is not totally reliable. Once you have gathered this information, define the range for the salary you want.

*Chapter 4*

# The Art of Negotiation:
# Eleven Proven Principles

# In This Chapter

1. Postpone the Negotiation

2. Avoid Mentioning Your Last Salary

3. Make *Them* Talk First

4. Keep Your Options Open

5. Up the Ante

6. Narrow the Gap

7. Negotiate Future Salary Increases

8. Avoid Bluffing

9. Stand Your Ground

10. No Telephone Negotiation—Ever!

11. Get It in Writing

Now that you have the right attitude, a good sense of timing, and a thorough understanding of salaries themselves, you're ready to begin negotiating. The following eleven principles will help bring the chances for a successful salary negotiation in your favor. The first and foremost principle of good negotiation, however, relates back to Chapter 2, reemphasizing the importance of timing when it comes to salary negotiation.

*Always postpone salary negotiation until the appropriate time. Even if you are asked a direct question related to salary, there are many ways to tactfully postpone the discussion until you are ready.*

*If the interviewer insists on discussing salary, you can always bounce the question back to him, asking him to speak on the issue first.*

# PRINCIPLE 1:
# POSTPONE THE NEGOTIATION

Never begin salary negotiation before receiving a firm job offer. If your interviewer mentions the salary issue at the beginning of the interview, you can respond with something like: "Thank you so much for mentioning this issue. Before we discuss this, may I ask you . . . ?"

This technique will move the conversation away from the salary issue. Ask questions regarding the responsibilities, the tasks, the mission of the job. If the interviewer has you "on the ropes" and will not be dissuaded from discussing the salary issue, do not lose your chance at a good job by refusing to discuss this issue. Instead, quote a very broad salary range or use one of the following four strategies to postpone salary negotiation.

**1. Bounce back the question to the interviewer.**
- "I am sure that you have budgeted an amount for this job. What sort of range does the salary curve or your budget show?"

#53

#54

*You can also use "stall tactics" to postpone discussion of salary without seeming rude or evasive.*

- "I have an idea of what the market offers for this type of job. Could we please begin by discussing what your company is prepared to offer?"

- "A company like yours surely has an idea of the salary range to be offered. What do your salary curves suggest?"

## 2. Stall Elegantly

- "I am sure we will come to a fair agreement on salary once we have established I am the right person for the job."

- "Salary isn't the issue here. I know that I have to produce more than I cost. First, let's figure out how much I will produce for you."

- "Salary is the third item on my working conditions list. First, let's establish that we can work together. Second, let me show you how, through my job/work I will contribute positively to your organization. Then, as a third point, we can discuss the salary issue."

## 55

*Humor is a good way to defuse the pressure to discuss salary prematurely.*

*Honesty and frankness can disarm your interviewer and redirect discussion away from salary.*

### 3. Use Your Sense of Humor

- "Your job as interviewer is to make me talk about salary! My job as interviewee is to remain silent on this issue! Isn't it?"

- "I never like to talk about salary for a job I am not sure is right for me. Could we first see if I am the right candidate for the job?"

- "What I expect from a job is far greater than what I expect from a salary!"

**#56**

### 4. Disarm Your Interviewer

- "Discussing the money issue at this stage of the interview is a little bit premature, don't you think?"

- "I hope you won't mind if I ask to postpone this discussion for now."

- "As a principle, I don't like to discuss salary prior to being offered a job. I'm sure you can understand that."

- "I'm sure the salary offered for this job will be fair, equitable, and satisfactory ."

**#57**

*Never mention your previous salary during a negotiation. It can undermine your leverage and give your interviewer an upper hand.*

# PRINCIPLE 2: AVOID MENTIONING YOUR LAST SALARY

There are at least five reasons why an interviewer wants to know your last salary or your salary expectations as soon as possible (preferably even before the interview). This knowledge allows him to:

- gauge where you fit in the salary range;

- screen you out quickly if the number of candidates is large, as salary is an ideal and obvious way to compare candidates and screen them out;

- save money if your actual or last salary is below the one budgeted for the job;

- know the market better;

- evaluate your level of entry into his company (competency ratio).

When reacting to a question regarding your actual (or last) salary, it is essential not to answer at all. One of these four tactics will help you.

*To avoid mentioning your salary, try giving only a broad range.*

*Quote informal company policies about nondisclosure of salary to avoid mentioning your salary.*

*Offer to disclose your current salary later—only after you have negotiated your new salary.*

**Tactic 1: Range.** When your interviewer asks you what your current/last salary is/was, give only a broad range:

> Q: *How much do you make in your present job?*
>
> A: **In my present job my salary is exactly in the range I'm shooting for now: between _____ and _____.**

**Tactic 2: Gentlemen's Agreement.** If you come from a company or work for an organization where there is a gentlemen's agreement about nondisclosure of salaries, seize this opportunity not to answer.

> Q: *How much do you make in your present job?*
>
> A: **At XYZ company, where I work now, there is a gentleman's agreement about non-disclosure of salary. I must stick to the moral commitment I made to them not to discuss my salary with anyone.**

**Tactic 3: Later Stage Disclosure.** This tactic consists of proposing to give the information to your interviewer at a later stage. This means you will disclose the

*Avoid mentioning your current salary by offering instead the projected salary you will make after your next promotion.*

information but only after you have negotiated a salary with him. This method is common in highly competitive fields, such as computer or telephone systems sales. When your interviewer asks you to tell him your current/previous salary, do it as described below.

**Q:** *How much do you make in your present job?*

**A:** **Would you like to see a copy of my last pay slip or should I just tell you my salary?**

**Q:** *No, just tell me.*

**A:** **Well, before I tell you I would like to negotiate my future salary with you. When we have an agreement, I will disclose my former salary.**

Your interviewer may then smile and tell you that you are a "tough negotiator." Simply thank him and say, "The toughness and style I bring to the negotiation table, I will bring to work for you full time in my new job!"

**Tactic 4: Anticipated Salary.** If you are presently in a job, this technique consists of telling the salary you will be making after your next promotion.

**#62**

*Force your interviewer to make the first offer: whoever mentions the first figure is usually at a disadvantage.*

Q: *How much do you make in your present job?*

A: **After my next promotion, which occurs in four months, my salary will be raised to _____.**

## PRINCIPLE 3: MAKE THEM TALK FIRST

In the good old Western movies, in the final duel scene, there was always a good guy and a bad guy. In the traditional movie, the bad guy was the first to move but the good guy always drew faster and shot the bad guy dead! The same thing happens in salary negotiation: The first one who makes a move, gets shot down! It is always best to talk last. Wait for the interviewer to expose himself. Effectively postponing the negotiation and making the interviewer talk first has several advantages. Most importantly you:

- get a better salary offer than you originally planned;

- refrain from "shooting yourself in the foot" by asking for too low a figure, or from ending the negotiation by asking for too high a figure;

#63

*When it comes to proposing the first salary figure, practice ways of throwing the ball back into your interviewer's court. Try rehearsing the sample dialogs in this book in front of a mirror.*

- "up the ante" more easily when salary is finally discussed later;

- take the necessary time to obtain specific information about the level of the job and its corresponding responsibilities;

- can gauge how the interviewer is evaluating you before you have to negotiate with him;

- discover the starting point of the negotiation process.

Sometimes an interviewer will try to open negotiations by coming right out and asking how much money you want to make. It is important not to take the bait and simply state a figure or a range. To keep the advantage, tactfully turn the question back on to your interviewer:

Q: *How much do you want to earn?*

A: **Oh, thank you for raising this issue. Before answering you, I'd like to ask a question.**

Q: *Please do.*

#64

*If an interviewer mentions a salary figure, do not agree or disagree; instead state that the figure "fits perfectly into my range." This way you keep your options open for later negotiation.*

A: **Do you have salary curves or indexes in your organization?**

Q: *Yes, of course we do.*

A: **Could you tell me, then, what sort of salary range you have in mind for this job, based on those curves? This will make things easier and save us time.**

# PRINCIPLE 4:
# KEEP YOUR OPTIONS OPEN

Sometimes the interviewer will mention salary early in the interview as if it were predetermined and nonnegotiable. He may say something like: "We have projected a salary of _____ for this job," or, "The final figure we have is _____." Although, in accordance with Principle 2, you will probably want to delay discussions of salary at this point, Principle 2 applies only when the interviewer is prematurely *wanting* you to discuss salary. In this case, he may be simply trying to slip a figure by you without further discussion. If you do not reply in some way, your silence could be taken as an

acceptance of the stated salary. If a figure is given, it is important not to simply nod in understanding or otherwise let the remark go by. This may foreclose your ability to negotiate later. Instead, you must acknowledge that the subject of salary has come up *without either agreeing or disagreeing* and then either 1) employ strategies to postpone further discussion, or 2) follow the strategy discussed below.

Sometimes, after stating a figure, the interviewer will ask, "Would that fit you?," "Do you agree?," or, "Is that the sort of range you are interested in?" Never simply say that you agree or disagree. Instead, simply state, "This figure fits perfectly into my range." This rather open-ended reply can accomplish several things:

- keep the discussion from getting stalled or stuck, or prematurely focused on salary;

- keep you from being tied solely to the amount the interviewer proposes;

- keep you from having to accept his offer;

- allow you to continue the interview with all your salary options open.

*Rehearse the sample dialog given here to practice reopening negotiations after you have agreed to a general salary range.*

Consider the following dialog to see how the interview might progress in this situation:

*Q: We have budgeted _____ for this job.*

**A: This figure fits perfectly into my range.**

Then you can proceed using facts and figures to show him that you are the right person for the job, listing achievements that match his needs. When you feel you are at the Plateau Stage (see Chapter 2), you are in a position to continue:

**A: Can we now negotiate my salary with your organization?**

*Q: We have already done it!*

**A: Yes, you already told me what sort of budget you have for this job and I told you that this figure fits exactly in my range. Now that I know what the job entails, I can better narrow down my range from _____ to _____.**

Now you can simply state your range and begin the negotiation. Make sure the lower figure of your range is close to the figure stated by the interviewer.

#66

*When your interviewer mentions the first salary figure, use the "Echo" method to up the ante.*

## PRINCIPLE 5: UP THE ANTE

## 67

If you have successfully postponed negotiation to the proper time, and if you have succeeded in making the interviewer mention the first figure, it is now your job to "up the ante." One very effective method is to use "The Echo."

"The Echo" is just what it sounds like: simply repeat the figure stated by the interviewer and then remain silent. Whatever amount is stated, do not show a reaction. Your face should remain calm and unchanged. The full technique looks like this:

1. Your interviewer has spoken first and mentioned a salary of _____. Repeat this figure exactly with only the slightest suggestion of a surprise or question.

2. Look the interviewer in the eyes, or if this embarrasses you, look at his eyebrows or the right or left side of his face.

3. Do not be overt. Do not show satisfaction or deception, only the faintest hint of a surprise.

*Use the sample dialogs given here to practice the "Echo" technique. Rehearsing with a friend will help you feel less awkward.*

4. The very fact that you repeat the amount and then remain silent, showing no other reaction, may cause the interviewer to be perplexed. As a result, he may increase his offer.

You will want to practice this technique because it can feel awkward. When a figure is mentioned, a reaction is expected, and your impulse will be to give one—either positive or negative. If you have rehearsed well, however, you can hold your emotions in check, and maintain a calm, cool silence after you have simply repeated the figure. It may feel awkward, but that's exactly why it's effective. Your interviewer will want to break the awkward silence—usually by suggesting a higher figure!

Here's an example of a dialog using the "Echo" technique:

A: **May I ask what sort of salary you have budgeted for this job?**

Q: *We have budgeted around 100.*

A: **100?…**

#68

*If the salary you want is higher than the one offered, try to fill that gap—and only that gap.*

Remain silent and wait for the interviewer to break the pause.

**Q: Yes, 100...but this is not our final offer!**

**A: This is not your final offer?...**

One last note: if the interviewer mentions a range instead of a flat figure, repeat the higher figure when using the Echo technique. It can be just as effective!

## PRINCIPLE 6: NARROW THE GAP

If the salary you desire is higher than the one being offered, try to fill that gap *and that gap only*. Furthermore, try to make the gap appear as small as possible. If you are speaking in terms of an annual salary, for example, divide the salary gap by 12 to make it a monthly figure, which appears smaller.

For instance, if you want an annual salary of 112 and you are offered 100, focus on the gap of 12 (112-100 = 12). Divide this yearly gap of 12 by 12 months, to get a monthly gap of one. This is then the place to begin your

#69

*During negotiation, find out the company's policy for future salary increases. That way, your future raises are also brought into the negotiation.*

negotiation: "Actually, we are very close to each other—our gap is only 1 per month. Can we see what we can do about this?"

# PRINCIPLE 7: NEGOTIATE FUTURE SALARY INCREASES

There are two types of increases for salaries: an *automatic* one to reflect a cost of living increase, and a *discretionary* one to reflect the merit of your performance or efficiency. Ask the interviewer one of the three following questions:

1. "As I hope to make my career with your organization, could you please let me know your policy for salary increases?"

2. "We have discussed the base salary. I am sure, in an organization like yours, there is a yearly adjustment to reflect a cost of living increase as well as a merit increase. Could you please elaborate on this?"

3. "I am very interested in the future I could have with your organization and would like you to elaborate

## 70

*Several good ways of negotiating future raises in your favor are discussed here. Learn them and practice them!*

on two points. First, when will the first raise be given? Second, will this raise reflect only a cost of living increase, or will it also include a merit adjustment?"

After you have asked this type of question, you must try to shorten the period until your first salary increase. This period should be as short as possible. There are three ways to shorten this timeframe, running from an "elegant understatement" to an ultimatum. Consider how the overall interview and negotiation has gone so far, and use your instinct to decide which tactic is best:

1. "Could we consider making the timeframe for a salary increase shorter than your usual policy?"

2. "The period between now and the first increase is long. By how many months could you shorten this?"

3. "I like your salary offer. However, I can only accept it if you are willing to give me a raise within _____ months."

## 71

*More often than not, bluffing will undermine your negotiation. Stick to smart strategies with a firm basis in fact.*

# PRINCIPLE 8: AVOID BLUFFING

A large majority of people believe it is hard to negotiate without some bluffing taking place. However, experience shows that the most successful negotiations are done without bluffing and are organized around very smart strategies of information retention.

You will be more efficient if you stick to the truth for several reasons:

#72

- the very fact that you use only true information makes you feel more comfortable and secure, which makes the interview easier for you;

- when checking is done after the interview, your integrity and good faith are proven and you benefit from this;

- bluffing, lies, or exaggeration can hamper the otherwise good negotiation tactics at your disposal and quite possibly close the door on an interesting job.

*Being firm and persistent can feel uncomfortable, but it will usually work in your favor. Be prepared to stand your ground.*

# PRINCIPLE 9: STAND YOUR GROUND

If you are firm and persistent, you may fear your interviewer will feel you are somewhat inflexible, but it is more likely he will respect your tenacity and self-confidence, which will only increase his esteem for you.

If, however, you feel embarrassed and wish to lighten the mood (humor has never hampered a good negotiation), you can try one of the four following strategies.

**1. Agree with Gentle Humor**

    Q: *You certainly are tough when it comes to negotiating!*

    A: Why, thank you!

**2. Turn Negatives to Positives**

    Q: *You seem so sure of yourself! It appears that nothing will make you budge.*

    A: Yes, this is a compliment given to me by many of my past employers.

*Humor, common sense, and friendly competitiveness are all good ways to defuse tension during an interview if neither side is backing down.*

### 3. Common Sense

Q: *You appear to be a person who is always watching out for himself.*

A: Do you think so?

Q: *Yes, you seem to be very interested in the money aspect of this job.*

A: The job to be filled requires excellent negotiation skills. I am demonstrating that I have those skills. Later, when I work for you, I will fight and negotiate just as firmly on your behalf.

### 4. One-Upmanship

Q: *As a negotiator, you are not what I would call easy.*

A: Oh, thank you! I am convinced that you are testing me right now. Shall we try arm wrestling too?

*Negotiating on the telephone puts you at a great disadvantage. Insist on discussing salary issues face to face.*

# PRINCIPLE 10: NO TELEPHONE NEGOTIATION—EVER!

**#75**

Turn down any proposal to negotiate salary over the telephone. Use the telephone only to confirm that you accept a firm job offer. All other details must be negotiated in person. Negotiating by phone has two main disadvantages:

- You cannot see your interviewer and therefore you cannot measure his interest (or indifference) to what you are saying.

- Your negotiation position is weaker and you are more vulnerable. If there is any type of mismatch, the split will be one that you cannot address again.

If, as sometimes happens, you feel that your interviewer is trying to renegotiate an already agreed-upon salary over the phone, adopt one of the two following attitudes:

- If you do not want to renegotiate, remain firm and say you do not wish to reconsider the previous offer.

*Get any job offer or salary proposal in writing. Promises can be vague, misunderstood, or unscrupulously "misremembered." The risks are too great, so clarify everything in writing.*

- If you are willing to reopen the negotiation, say that—as a principle—you never negotiate money issues over the phone and arrange for an immediate appointment.

## PRINCIPLE 11: GET IT IN WRITING

Accepting a firm job offer together with a salary proposal can be done either verbally or in writing. However, a confirmation in writing is a *must* in the following four cases:

- if you have some sort of negative intuition or feeling about your interviewer and have doubts about the value of his word;

- if the promises made to you seem too numerous or generous to be given without something more being demanded of you some time down the road;

- if the salary formula is complex (due to adjustments, commissions, etc.), or if you think the salary has not been stated clearly or not negotiated thoroughly enough;

• if the risk to you is great. For instance, if you must resign from a present job to take a new job the risk is too large to accept without having a firm written proposal in your hand, signed by the person for whom you will actually be working.

If the interviewer is reluctant to commit in writing, suggest that you write the letter for him to sign, saying, "How do you want to proceed? Do you plan to confirm this offer in writing yourself or would you prefer that I do it?"

If the new employer agrees that you should write the letter, be sure to stress the interest you have for the job and exactly what has been agreed upon by the two of you. Send your new employer two copies, signed by you. Ask him to sign one and return it to you in an enclosed stamped self-addressed envelope.

*Chapter 5*

# The Nitty-Gritty:
# Seven Specific Strategies

# In This Chapter

1. A Piece of the Pie

2. The Trampoline

3. Partial Time

4. Multiple Offers

5. Job Switching Bonus

6. Range

7. Survey

Now that you are familiar with the general principles of salary negotiation, here are seven specific strategies that can be used. Many of them can be used in any situation, and a few are appropriate in only certain situations. Each section lists advantages and disadvantages for the strategy. Weigh these considerations against your particular situation to decide which approach is best for you. Alternatively, depending on your circumstances, you may be able to combine strategies, taking certain ideas or elements from several sections. These strategies have all been used successfully by other job hunters, but if they inspire new ideas for your own approach, don't hesitate to be creative!

*One good negotiation strategy is to quantify your contribution—then ask for a piece of the pie!*

## 77

# STRATEGY 1: A PIECE OF THE PIE

*Figure out the impact of your work
in terms of financial contribution
and ask for a share of it.*

Through your work you will contribute positively to:

- the increase of profits/gains;
- the decrease of costs/expenses;
- the avoidance of mistakes/errors.

Figure out your salary in relationship to the contribution you will generate. Use your past achievements, information you have gathered from your research, and whatever you learn from your interviewer to quantify the contribution of your work. Measure this contribution by yourself or with your interviewer. Once you reach an approximate amount, state it and ask him to pay you part of it as a salary (one-fifth, one-fourth, one-third, half, etc.). The negotiation might resemble the following dialog:

*Q: How much do you want to make?*

**A: Thank you for asking. I have figured out
the contribution I could make to your**

department /organization. In a previous job, I reduced costs by _____ and increased sales by _____.These types of achievements should be transferable to your department/organzation. Hence, my salary could be based in part on a share of this contribution.

## Advantages of this Strategy

- You stick to the economic reality.

- You stand apart from other candidates—you are unique.

- Your calculations are objective and rational.

- Your salary will automatically be adjusted on your future performance.

- You do not have to mention your current or previous salary.

- You avoid negative comparisons with figures from salary curves.

- Your salary may be more easily renegotiated in the future.

*The Piece of the Pie strategy is especially useful if you do work that is easily quantifiable, but if this strategy appeals to you, you can usually find a way to measure your contribution.*

### Disadvantages of this Strategy

- The calculation is not always easy or possible.
- You do not use traditional methods to talk about salary, which may puzzle your interviewer.
- Your reasoning will probably depart from salary curves.
- You may be penalized if the results of your work are not satisfactory.
- Your calculations may, in some instances, lead to negative results.
- Your salary may be open to continual review.

### Advice for Using this Strategy

This strategy is by far the simplest and most efficient one. It is, of course, the easiest one to use for those who do work that has immediate, tangible, and visible results (applied research, sales, production, etc.). It appears more difficult to use for some jobs. However, upon reflection, there is always a quantifiable way to measure the impact of work in an organization.

#78

*When negotiations are at a stalemate, accept a lower offer on the condition that you will receive a substantial raise after a short trial period.*

# STRATEGY 2: THE TRAMPOLINE

*Accept a job with lower pay than
you expected but with a written commitment
of a substantial raise in the near future
(3 to 6 months).*

#79

If the figure you have in mind does not correspond to the one stated by your interviewer—say you want a monthly salary of 80 and his figure is 60—use this strategy.

After all figures are stated (namely, 80 and 60), remain silent for a time, reflect, and then offer a counterproposal. The proposal consists of accepting his 60 offer with one condition: your salary will be readjusted after an initial period (sometimes linked to objectives) and will be retroactive to your start date.

It is a good sign if the interviewer starts talking about the retroactive component of the proposal. This means he has accepted the principle of going from 60 to 80 and is now discussing the details. You may show flexibility on the details because you have already been successful in getting him to jump from 60 to 80 (the key issue).

Of course, this type of agreement must be confirmed in writing prior to joining the organization. The negotiation might look something like the following dialog.

> *Q: How much do you want to make?*
>
> **A: 80 per month.**
>
> *Q: I'm sorry, but this figure goes far beyond the one we have budgeted.*
>
> **A: May I ask what you have budgeted?**
>
> *Q: 60 per month.*

Remain silent for a while, and then continue:

> **A: I really want to work for you. Therefore, let me suggest this. I will start at 60, and within six months, if we are both satisfied, you raise me to 80 with a retroactive effect.**

### Advantanges of this Strategy

- You show your commitment, determination, and good faith.

- You test the level of trust your interviewer has for you.

- You make your interviewer feel secure about you.

*Do not use the Trampoline strategy if the nature of your work exposes you to the risk of unscrupulous conduct.*

- You get what you want without having made a major concession.

- You stress the fact that this type of contract has two winners.

### Disavantages of this Strategy

- You agree to make less money for a few months.

- Your benefits are calculated on a lower monthly basis.

- You could fail during the initial trial period due to factors beyond your control.

### Advice for Using this Strategy

This strategy should not be used in jobs where contributions or results can be stolen by unscrupulous employers and co-workers during the initial trial period. Examples might include a salesperson whose customer list could be "borrowed," a researcher who could lose a specific technology, or a production foreman who could disclose his own techniques for more efficient productivity.

#80

*If they can pay you only part of what you want, offer to give only part of your time. This type of arrangement is increasingly common within certain industries in today's job market. Just because it's nontraditional, don't be afraid to suggest it!*

# STRATEGY 3: PARTIAL TIME

*Offer to work on a part-time basis if they cannot pay you the salary you want.*

Sometimes you will be attracted by a specific job or company. However, the company you are interested in may not have the financial resources to offer you the salary you want. If this is the case, offer to work part time and have them pay you the amount forecasted for a full-time job.

Let's say you want a monthly salary of 100 and their figure is 60. After all figures are stated (namely, 100 and 60), remain silent for a time, reflect, and then offer a counterproposal. The proposal consists of agreeing to work for the salary stated by the interviewer, but limiting the working time to a portion of full-time hours. In the case of a 40-hour work week, you could suggest approximately 24 hours (40 x 60 divided by 100). Once you have a job which uses 60 percent of your time, it is up to you to find a second employer who can pay you for the remaining 40 percent.

*When negotiating a part-time arrangement, offer a percentage of your time, rather than a certain work schedule. This way you get what you want, but keep your work schedule more flexible.*

This type of agreement is very common in some fields and for some types of jobs, including training centers, nonprofit organizations dealing with social issues, and accountants.

If you accept this type of arrangement, it is essential that you do not spend more than the portion of time agreed (in our example, 60 percent) on their premises. If you have to deal with a very heavy workload or have to work overtime to face the challenge you accepted, take the work home. Do not do it at your work location. This will allow you to maintain a strong position when it is time to renegotiate your contract. When you elect to work part time in this way, you are not allowing yourself to be underpaid. The employer is not allowed to pay 60 percent for 90 percent of your time, and you have avoided setting a precedent with which you are unprepared to live.

During this negotiation it is better to use percentages of time rather than days. Do not say "half time" or "three-quarters time." Say "60 percent of my time" rather than "three days per week," or "50 percent of my time" rather than "two-and-a-half days per week" or "half time." This allows you to determine the way time is split

#82

after you have negotiated the amount you will be paid. For instance, 60 percent of the time could correspond to either three days a week or thirteen days per month.

The negotiation for this arrangement might look something like the following dialog.

> *Q: I am sorry, but we cannot offer you the salary of 100 that you want. Our means are limited and the figure you suggest is out of our range.*
>
> A: **What sort of salary did you budget?**
>
> *Q: 60 per month.*

Remain silent for awhile, and then continue:

> A: **I must admit that your organization attracts me, and I want to work for you. In addition, the job we discussed corresponds exactly to the type of work I want and to which I can contribute. So let me suggest the following: I'll accept 60 per month but will only work 60 percent of my time.**

### Advantages of this Strategy

• You do not lose a job that really interests you.

- By having two or three employers, you spread the risk and don't put "all your eggs into one basket."

- You will likely work more efficiently if you know your time on the employer's premises is limited.

- You prove that this type of contract has two winners.

- If there is a work overload, you can renegotiate your contract (time and salary).

- You get the feeling you are really needed.

## Disadvantages of this Strategy

- In the beginning, sharing your time with two or three employers can create feelings of insecurity and uneasiness.

- You may feel that you do not have enough time to delve deeply into the problems/needs of any one of your employers.

- Your financial situation may be difficult and uncertain at times.

*If your interviewer is skeptical of a part-time arrangement, offer to work full time for a period while you "learn the ropes."*

- You may lose credibility with colleagues, or they may be envious.

- It may appear that you are receiving special treatment, which can elicit responses from colleagues that impair your ability to work efficiently.

**Advice for Using this Strategy**

Occasionally an interviewer will be interested in this type of proposal but will be skeptical that you can master the tasks and do the work with only 60 percent of your time devoted to him. In this case, offer to work a trial period during which you will be paid the 60, but you will work full time (for two to six weeks). At the conclusion of this trial period, you will drop back to part time (60 percent), after proving you have mastered the job. An alternative strategy is to work the equivalent of a five-day week and to include Saturday. In this way, you can bill one weekday to another company.

#83

*You can use other job offers as negotiation leverage by stating the highest offer you've received. Be careful of bluffing, however: you don't want to seem like you're blackmailing your interviewer!*

# STRATEGY 4: MULTIPLE OFFERS

*If you have other job offers, tell your interviewer about them. Then, if appropriate, state the highest salary you have been offered.*

Let's say you have established that you are the right person for the job. Your interviewer suddenly asks you how much money you want to make. You state that you are actively looking for a job and have two firm job offers under consideration. Watch out, no bluffing! Stick to the truth. Advise the interviewer of the highest salary amount offered to you. Immediately after this discussion, reassure your interviewer by telling him that if he were to offer you the same salary, you would, without hesitation, accept his offer. Do not say this if you do not mean it, otherwise you may come across as a blackmailer.

Then remain silent. Wait for him to break the silence and make a counteroffer.

The negotiation might look something like the following dialog.

*Q: How much do you want to make?*

A: As I mentioned to you earlier, I am actively looking for a job. I am now in the final phase, as I have already received two firm job offers. One of them has offered a salary of _____.

*Q: I take it there is some fierce competition out there!*

A: Yes, to a certain extent. However, if your organization can match this offer—or beat it—I'll decide on the spot. Of the three, I would immediately accept yours, because I like your organization very much. The job suits me and corresponds exactly to my skills. Also, I'd like to work for someone like you.

**Advantages of this Strategy**

- By stating that you have other job offers, you stress the fact that you are a resource person for others, thereby "up-ing the ante."

- You behave in a very natural and honest way by putting all your cards on the table.

- You provide your interviewer with information about the job market. This may help him—if

*Using multiple job offers can be an effective strategy: the less eager you are perceived (without appearing disinterested or lacking enthusiasm), the more desirable you become. A person with many options will not be seen as desperate!*

necessary—to have tangible information to justify offering you a salary higher than the one budgeted.

## Drawbacks of this Strategy

- You may anger your interviewer by being perceived as arrogant or boastful.
- You may generate a "no" or stall negotiations if your interviewer believes you are bluffing.
- You lose credibility if the strategy doesn't work and you accept their proposal on their terms.

## Advice for Using this Strategy

Avoid bluffing when you use this strategy. Do not say you have other offers if this is not the case. It is always easy to get a firm offer for a job you do not want. There are thousands of jobs out there that no one wants to do. Experience shows that the less eager you are perceived (without appearing disinterested or lacking enthusiasm), the more desirable you become. If your interviewer wants to know the names of the organizations that have made you offers, you should be specific

*If someone tries to lure you from your present job, do not disclose your current salary before they understand you will not change jobs unless they can offer the percentage salary increase you desire.*

and disclose them if it is helpful to you. If you do not want to disclose the names, decline in a tactful way by saying, "For obvious reasons, and to respect the wishes of these organizations, I must be discreet and not disclose their names."

# STRATEGY 5: JOB SWITCHING BONUS

*If someone tries to lure you from your present job, negotiate a job switching bonus.*

**#86**

Let's say that while in your current job, you are approached directly or indirectly by a headhunter, recruiting agency, or someone from another organization. They ask you to leave your present job and join a new company. To begin, state your satisfaction with your present job, while letting him know you are willing to discuss new opportunities that will further your career.

Secondly, tell them that you are happy where you are, and that you will not consider any professional move that does not increase your salary by at least _____ percent (anywhere from 10 to 50 percent). Your interviewer will then try to get you to disclose your present salary by

*Practice the sample dialog on negotiating with a headhunter. It's always best to rehearse how you will handle an unexpected situation before it happens.*

stating that this percentage is meaningless if he doesn't know your actual salary.

State that your current salary is already a "sure bet," and reiterate, on the other hand, the increase of _____ percent could result in an amount which could justify a move. After discussing and establishing this increase as a must, disclose your actual salary and use it as a springboard for further discussions.

The negotiation might look something like the following dialog.

> *Q: How much do you want to make?*
>
> A: **Thank you for raising the issue. As I told you, I like the job I am in right now, but I'm open to discussion. I will not consider a job change unless my salary were to increase by at least _____ percent.**
>
> *Q: Yes, I understand. This depends on your current salary, of course.*
>
> A: **For you, certainly. But for me, my current salary is 100 percent certain right now. The only variable for me is the potential salary increase I can make. It is important that we agree on this percentage before talking further.**

## 87

*Q: Okay. Let's assume a 20 percent increase.*

**A:** My actual salary is 100. Therefore, I would need a salary of 120 to leave my current job and join your organzation.

## Advantages of this Strategy

- If you are truly satisfied with your current job, you are at little risk.

- You use a very simple method—easy to substantiate and calculate.

- You improve your salary situation.

- You get feedback on your present job.

- You may be able to use this counteroffer in your present organization to better your position.

- You feel that you are valuable to others.

- You project the image of a serious, determined person.

## Disadvantages of this Strategy

- You may be perceived as someone only interested in money and not the content of the job.

- You may come across as too demanding and become less desirable.

- You take the risk of moving to a job which does not match your other needs.

## Advice for Using this Strategy

The difficulty is to determine the percentage increase you want. It is best to state two figures (a range of 20 to 40 percent), instead of just one (30 percent). The appropriate percentage also varies according to the market situation: eagerness of competition, unemployment rate, the demand for your skills. Take these considerations into account when deciding what percentage is appropriate.

*If you've done your homework, you can safely state a salary range that spans from the highest salaries of your subordinates to the salary of the person directly above you.*

# STRATEGY 6: RANGE

*State a range from the (highest) salaries of your future subordinates to the salary of the person to whom you will report.*

## 88

Ask your interviewer to provide you with information about the people who will work for you. Ask him about their motivations, their experience, their backgrounds, and their average salary, and ask him to specify the highest salary paid. Then change the subject. You now have an indication of the lowest part of your salary range and the figure below which you cannot, under any circumstances, go.

Also, during the interview, try to evaluate the salary of the person to whom you will report: probably your boss, manager, or supervisor. The research you performed on the company to prepare for the interview will help you identify who this person is likely to be. This information, along with research from salary surveys for companies of similar size in similar fields, can help you determine what your manager's salary is likely to be.

As a general rule, your boss will make anywhere from 25 to 50 percent more than you, and possibly 50 to 100 percent more than your subordinates. When the end of the interview is approaching and you are asked your salary expectations, state a range that runs from the salary of the best paid subordinate (as your lower end) to the probable salary of your superior (as your upper end).

The conversation might resemble the following dialog.

*Q: How much do you want to make?*

A: Thank you for raising this issue. Before we discuss my figures I wonder if you could give me some details about the people who will work for me?

*Q: Certainly. What would you like to know?*

A: I'd like some information about what they think about their jobs, whether they like them, their motivations, their professional tracks, their skills, backgrounds …

*Q: There are seven people who would work for you. Most of them have a background in _____ …*

A: **And from a salary standpoint, do they consider themselves well paid or underpaid?**

Q: *No, I believe that our salaries are in line with the rest of the market.*

A: **What is the highest salary any one of them makes?**

Q: *100 per month.*

A: **Thank you for the information.**

Then, later in the interview, when the conversation turns back to salary negotiation:

Q: *Could you tell me how much you want to make?*

Remember that the best paid person among your subordinates makes 100, and that your research has allowed you to estimate the probable salary of your superior at 180. You are now safe to answer:

A: **Yes, with pleasure. Now that I have specific information about the job, I can answer you. First, let me tell you that I like your organization and would certainly enjoy working here. As far as my salary, my range runs from 130 to 160.**

**Advantages of this Strategy**

- You discover the salary policy of the organization.

- You measure the knowledge your interviewer has about his organization.

- You get a feeling for the communication policy of your future organization if you take the job.

- You risk little in your salary negotiation because your range is calculated by reasonable and proven figures.

- You use figures which do not create precedents and fit in with existing company salary curves.

**Disadvantages of this Strategy**

- The salaries of your subordinates are not necessarily a good benchmark for the lower end of your range.

- You may make your interviewer uncomfortable by requesting information often considered taboo (the salaries of others).

- You expose yourself to questions about your last salary.

- You may be perceived as placing too much importance on the salary issue.

- You may be provided with erroneous figures.

- The figures you state may bear no relationship to your skills, and reflect only existing salary curves, which may be out of sync with other companies in the same field.

- The top of your range is often a figure based only on an educated guess and may pose a risk to you.

**Advice for Using this Strategy**

This is a very useful method and easy to use, especially when salaries are published. If this strategy appeals to you, be sure to perform the necessary research before the interview.

*You may be able to justify your salary expectations based on information you've gained from salary surveys. Be sure to tell your interviewer why the particular surveys you quote are appropriate (they are for salaries in the same industry, in the same geographical area, for companies of similar sizes, etc.)*

# STRATEGY 7: SURVEY

## 89

*If the information you gather from salary surveys is favorable to you, share this information with your interviewer.*

Prior to going to your interview, consult the most recent salary surveys conducted in your field for the type of job you desire. You will find them in magazines, newspapers, professional associations, alumni associations, government reports, or on the Internet.

During the interview, when asked for your salary figure, quote the surveys. Tell the interviewer how and when the surveys were conducted and published. Then quote the figures or ranges that correspond to the job for which you have applied.

Your dialog might look like this:

**Q: *What are your salary expectations?***

**A: Thank you for asking. Before our meeting today, I took time to gather some information, and I studied a survey conducted by the XYZ Institute. It covers salaries paid in this area by organizations of your size in this**

*Don't rely on surveys too much. They do nothing to make you stand out from other candidates. Be sure to supply plenty of justifications for your salary expectations that are based on your unique skills and experience as well.*

field. From this survey it appears that someone with my credentials and background in the job of _____ has a salary between 85 and 100.

## Advantages of this Strategy

- The figures you state are published and difficult to question.
- You do not commit yourself personally.
- You provide a range without limiting yourself to one figure.
- You state facts and figures, which is very reassuring to an interviewer.

## Disadvantages of this Strategy

- You place yourself in comparison to others—as just "one of many."
- You do not define yourself in relationship to your skills and competencies, but according to characteristics that have little, if anything, to do with your potential.

#90

- Your survey may be questioned if it does not apply to the field or the size of the organization with which you are negotiating.

**Advice for Using this Strategy**

Of course, use only those surveys that are favorable to you!

*Chapter 6*

# "Raising" the Bar

# In This Chapter

It Takes the Right Attitude

Timing Is Everything

The Nuts and Bolts of Asking for a Raise

The Nitty-Gritty:
The Five Steps of Asking for a Raise

Seven Strategies
to Prove You Should Earn More

Eight Ways to "Up the Ante" in Your Favor

So, you think you have done the hard part? You have found yourself a great job, managed to negotiate a fair compensation package, and now can just coast along without worry? Wrong! It is never too early to think about how you can better your circumstances when the time is right. This doesn't mean that you should begin scheming for a raise the second day on the job, but it does mean that you should begin to understand and prepare for the day when you will want to approach your boss to discuss better compensation. You will need to be clear about the best time to discuss an increase, the nature of the increase, and a strategy to position yourself in the best way possible to prove you have earned it.

*Just as with salary negotiation, it is up to you to supply concrete reasons that you deserve a raise. Don't assume that you simply have a right to a raise.*

## IT TAKES THE RIGHT ATTITUDE

As we stated in the beginning of this book, attitude determines how well you will do in any endeavor. You often hear the following kinds of statements when it comes to raises:

- Employers do not give salary increases, employees earn them.

- You have no right to an increase, you have to earn it.

- You have the right to a salary adjustment due to inflation or an increase in the cost of living, but you have no right to an increase based on merit.

If the above statements are true, it is up to you, and you alone, to show your boss exactly why you deserve an increase. To do this you must know when enough time has passed to begin this kind of discussion, as well as what type of increase you want and are entitled to get.

#91

*The best times to negotiate a raise are 1) when you have received praise for a job well done, and 2) when you have taken on a significant number of new responsibilities or tasks.*

# TIMING IS EVERYTHING

How much time should pass before you should think about your next salary increase? If you have agreed with your employer during negotiation that you would work for a specific amount of time and then qualify for an increase, be sure to remind them of this issue a month before the time the higher salary should go into effect. This notice will allow for any unresolved issues to be cleared up in preparation for paying the higher salary.

If you did not have this type of agreement, the time to begin reflecting upon a salary increase is now—the moment you are hired, or as soon as you received your last raise. Don't expect that your employer will automatically reward your performance. You must demonstrate that your performance is of a consistently high quality to prove to your boss that you deserve a raise. As we'll discuss, there are strategies that you can begin using immediately to ensure that your achievements are noticed. Then it is up to you to ask for a salary adjustment. The two best times to do it are the following:

1. when praised for work you have just completed;
2. when major changes occur in your job responsibilities or tasks.

#92

*Before asking for a raise, be very clear how much you want. Then, if you are offered a lower increase, you may decide to turn it down. Turning down a salary increase may make your employer more generous next time.*

# THE NUTS AND BOLTS OF ASKING FOR A RAISE

There are two types of salary increases:

- an automatic revision to reflect an increase in the cost of living;

- an increase to reflect your merit or to compensate for your performance for efficiency.

By focusing on these two parameters, you can increase your salary/benefits. Be sure you understand if you are talking about a cost of living increase only, a merit increase, or both. When you finally open the subject with your boss, have your homework done and approach him with two firm objectives:

**1. Be very clear on the amount of increase you want.** Find out what the standard cost of living raise is and be prepared to ask for at least the minimum amount. To be worth the effort, a merit salary increase should be from 5 to 15 percent of your existing salary. Set a minimum level under which you will not accept the increase. When you turn down an increase you may

## 93

*When discussing a raise, agree upon a timeframe for it to take effect. Allow enough time for your employer to adequately consider and implement the increase.*

cause your employer to become concerned that you will leave. This will likely make him more generous the next time.

**2. Set a time period for this increase to take effect.** If you want an increase in one month, you will likely get it in one month. If you want it in one quarter, you will likely get it in one quarter. Prepare to discuss an increase with your employer in a timeframe that will allow him to consider it sufficiently and still begin when you wish.

#94

*Know the company policy on salary increases before asking for a raise. If there is a time schedule for raises, don't expect to be the exception. In other words, time your negotiation appropriately.*

# THE NITTY-GRITTY: THE FIVE STEPS OF ASKING FOR A RAISE

You've been at the job for six months or a year and you are ready to ask for a raise. What do you do now?

**Step One: Timing.** Establish that you are not jumping the gun. If you work for a company or agency that has annual performance and salary reviews, do not expect that you will be the exception for an increase in six months! In many hiring interviews, the time that an increase can be discussed has already been determined and agreed upon. Honor any agreement you have made in your hiring interview, unless your employer tells you that they would like to discuss an increase before that time arrives (and thank your lucky stars!) Know the company policy and know if your contribution will allow for you to discuss an increase at times other than those already established. If there is no company policy on this issue and you feel you have performed above expectations or have recently been given new responsibilities, you may want to broach the subject with your boss.

#95

*Be as concrete as possible about your contributions and achievements when negotiating a raise. Come to the table armed with specific information about your positive impact on the organization.*

**Step Two: Amount.** Establish the amount or percentage of increase you want before beginning any discussion with your boss. Your suggested increase must be fair and reasonable to your employer and must be able to be justified by your contribution. If you ask for a 30 percent raise after six months without some major facts to justify it, you will accomplish two things you don't want: you will not get the raise, and you will likely show your employer that you are a person who cannot be trusted to make good judgments. If, on the other hand, you have increased profits by $200,000 in less than one year, you can risk asking for a larger-than-normal increase, and you will be respected as a person who knows his own value.

**Step Three: Be Armed with Information.** Establish your contribution by outlining the ways you have excelled at your job. Take the logs you have been keeping with your achievements and ideas to the meeting (see page 211). Show exactly how you have increased profitability or effectiveness. Show exactly how you have decreased loss and errors. Never attend a meeting where you are asking for increased compensation without showing at least six concrete ways you deserve it!

#96

*When scheduling a meeting with your boss to discuss a raise, be sure to ask for enough time to cover the subject adequately. You will get only one shot to make your case. If you feel rushed, you might forget to talk about something important.*

**Step Four: Set Up the Meeting.** Only after the first, second, and third steps are completed should you set up a meeting with your employer to discuss a salary increase. You should ask for a meeting with the person(s) responsible for your position at a time that's both convenient to them and that still allows you to have a decision about an increase in the timeframe you desire. If you know that you wish to have your raise effective in one month, you should try to schedule the meeting at least six to eight weeks in advance of that time. This allows for your employer to think matters over and set in motion the procedures needed to allow your increase to take effect. Select the time of day that you know is the best time for your boss, which might include after regular business hours. Ask for enough time for make your case well; if you feel rushed you might forget to talk about something important. You may need to negotiate this raise so be sure you are prepared with the absolute minimum amount that you are willing to accept. Finish the meeting by outlining what has been covered and who will be responsible for the next step. If you need to get your terms in writing, establish who will be responsible for writing the agreement.

*If the negotiation doesn't go your way, establish with your boss specific criteria you will be judged on in the future. This will outline agreed-upon goals for you to work on—and bring to the negotiation table next time!*

**Step Five: If It Doesn't Go Your Way.** In the event the meeting does not have the outcome you desire and you are not given a raise (or too small a raise), thank your employer for meeting with you and remain polite. Try to establish what you need to do in the future to ensure you do get the raise you want. Outline with your boss the criteria you will be judged on, so you have exact and specific goals and priorities you can work toward. Write down the expectations your boss has of you so that there can be no misunderstanding the next time you meet. Clear up any problems that have existed in the past so they are not repeated. Leave the meeting knowing what you can do to become a better employee.

Finally, if you feel that you were denied an increase (or offered too little) for unfair or unjust reasons, and there is little hope that you will be happy if you remain with your employer, you may need to think about the next job you will seek!

#98

*Implement strategies to increase your visibility and highlight your achievements on a daily basis. When you do ask for a raise, there will be no question that you have been active and productive.*

# SEVEN STRATEGIES
# TO PROVE YOU SHOULD EARN MORE

Your "visibility" is essential to justify your demand for a salary increase. Understand and use all the means at your disposal to make sure you are "seen." It is essential that your work record and results are at the highest level prior to the time you request an increase.

Remember you are generally not observed eight hours a day, five days a week, by your boss. He is often unaware of your performance and the results you have achieved. You must therefore tell him (as well as the other members of the organization) your most important accomplishments.

To maintain or increase your visibility, here are nine ideas:

- Communicate your results to your boss verbally and in writing. Send him regular updates of your activities and underline major ones.

- Be active and be seen during working events and exhibitions, without stifling others.

- Accept speaking engagements where you represent your organization. Be sure to inform your boss when you do this.

- Write papers or articles promoting your division/organization.

- Become an expert witness, if appropriate, in your field of competency.

- Try to be quoted in print for the work you have done (get your name in the paper). To achieve this, approach journalists and provide them with nonconfidential information for an article. Provide them with press releases.

- Give conferences or courses at colleges, universities, professional associations, training centers, or community centers in your field of expertise.

*Set your priorities and shape your work habits in such a way that, when the time comes, your chances for a larger salary adjustment are increased.*

# EIGHT WAYS TO "UP THE ANTE" IN YOUR FAVOR

Here are some more tips that have proven successful at increasing your chances for a larger salary adjustment.

**#100**

- Identify what your department/division/boss needs the most—and then let him know you have done it.

- Select the achievements and missions that are essential and of most importance to your boss and carry them out in priority. Make sure the achievements you carry out are important to him and not just to you.

- Identify two or three tasks your boss dislikes and ask to do them for him.

- Get results that are beyond what is usually expected for the job.

- Do your work as if you had already received the increase you desire.

- Work, behave, and dress at the level of your boss.

*Each week, log the achievements, suggestions, and ideas you have contributed. When the time comes to negotiate a raise, you'll be glad you did!*

## 101

- Keep a private log of your achievements. Every week spend five minutes jotting down the most important tasks and results you achieved during the week.

- Keep a log of all suggestions and ideas you have discovered and/or implemented to improve productivity.

# About the Authors

A leading pioneer in career design and job hunting for over 25 years, **Daniel Porot** is an internationally recognized career expert. Daniel received his MBA in 1966 from the leading business school in Europe, Insead, and began his career with Exxon and Amoco before starting his own business in 1971.

He has authored more than a dozen best-selling French-language career books, translated Richard N. Bolles's *What Color is Your Parachute?* into French, and written *The PIE Method for Career Success* and *101 Toughest Interview Questions…And Answers that Win the Job!* for U.S. audiences.

In addition, he has personally trained more than 12,000 job hunters and 600 career counselors, and his training materials have been used by over two million job hunters worldwide. For twenty years, Daniel taught an annual two-week workshop with Richard Bolles.

He lives in Geneva, Switzerland, with his wife and four children.

**Frances Bolles Haynes** has worked in the field of career development for over twenty years. She began her career in Phoenix, helping CETA participants find employment. She then moved to Jackson, Mississippi, where she set up a successful job-hunting program based on the Job Club model, pioneered by Nathan Azrin.

She has worked with Daniel Porot for many years and is the coauthor of *101 Toughest Interview Questions…And Answers that Win the Job!* She has also served on the training staff of Richard Bolles. She is thankful to them both for their wisdom and genius.

Frances lives in Newport Beach, California, with her husband, Peter, and son, Donald.

Visit the authors' Web site at *www.careergames.com*. It is the most comprehensive and playful site in the career design and job hunting fields. There you will find career development exercises, games, and advice—all for free.